First published in Belgium and Holland by Clavis Uitgeverij, Hasselt – Amsterdam, 2008
Copyright © 2008, Clavis Uitgeverij

English translation from the Dutch by Clavis Publishing Inc. New York
Copyright © 2014 for the English language edition: Clavis Publishing Inc. New York

Visit us on the web at www.clavisbooks.com

Teachers and What They Do written and illustrated by Liesbet Slegers
Original title: De juf
Translated from the Dutch by Clavis Publishing

ISBN 978-1-60537-180-1

This book was printed in February 2014 at Proost, Everdongenlaan 23, 2300 Turnhout, Belgium

First Edition
10 9 8 7 6 5 4 3 2 1

Teachers
and What They Do

Liesbet Slegers

Clavis

NEW YORK

We go to school to learn all kinds of things.

When we're doing arts and crafts, we learn to use our hands.

When we're reading, writing, or doing sums,

we learn to use our heads.

Our teacher is the one who teaches us all those things.

Great, isn't it?

chalkboard

Our teacher wears regular clothes, not a uniform.
And that is how it should be, that's how we like her best.
Sometimes she uses chalk to draw on the board in front of the class
so we can all see clearly. When she is finished,
one of us is allowed to wipe the blackboard clean with a duster.
And sometimes she brings fun games in her book bag.

Piece
of chalk

Duster

Book bag

words and numbers

In the big children's classroom, there is a board on the wall.

The teacher writes letters, words, and numbers on it.

The big children learn to write in books.

They each have their own desk and chair.

All the classes have a bookcase full of books.

In our classroom there is also a huge closet

full of craft materials. We love making a mess!

Blackboard

Desks and chairs

Composition books

Craft materials

In the morning, when school begins, our teacher is all set.

She is waiting just for us at the school gates.

"Good morning, Miss," we say

before we enter the school grounds.

"Hello! Did you sleep well?" our teacher asks cheerfully.

Our teacher shows us how to do lots of arts and crafts.

She reads to us from funny books and exciting books.

She lets us play in the sand box,

the doll corner and the games corner.

And there is so much more to do....

The big kids have to sit still more than we do.

In their classroom, the teacher writes big letters

on the board, or numbers from 1 to 10.

She asks them questions to find out if they are paying attention.

"I know the answer, I know the answer!"

someone shouts proudly with his hand up in the air.

Our teacher also teaches gymnastics. Up we go,

on the balance beam and the rings.

This is fun. We all run around the room.

Sometimes our whole class goes swimming

in the big pool.

We learn to swim properly there, without swimming aids!

Our teacher is our friend. We can tell her everything.

When there's an argument, she sorts it out.

She always says we have to be nice to each other.

Our teacher comforts us when we are hurt or sad.

And she gives the really naughty kids time outs!

Not every school day is the same.

When someone has a birthday, we have a party.

And sometimes we go on field trips.

Then we are away from school all day!

Our teacher has taken us to the forest, the beach, and the zoo.

Sometimes our teacher has to work after school hours.

At home, she creates new lessons and looks for ideas.

She has to work on the computer, or to check homework.

She is very busy.

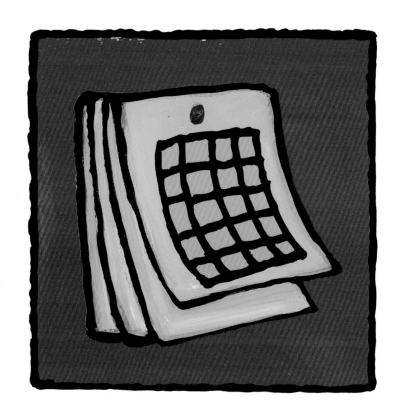

At the end of the school year, teachers deserve something nice.
We give our teacher a big hug and a small gift.
We thank her for a great year and wish her a fun
summer holiday.

Make a present for

1

Make a crown for your teacher.
Take a big piece of drawing paper and cut it
lengthwise, so you have two long strips.

2
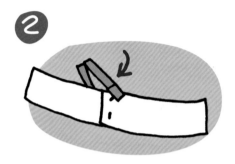
Staple the two strips together,
so you have one long strip of paper.

5

Boys: ask an adult to pour
some finger-paint in a dish.

6

Now print hands in different colors
all over the crown.
Do you want colorful kisses on
the crown too? See steps 3 and 4.

your teacher

3 Girls: put lipstick on your lips
(with your mommy's help).

4 Now put lipstick kisses all over the crown.
Do you want colored hands on the crown too?
See steps 5 and 6.

7 Use other nice materials
to decorate the crown.
Make it a real work of art!

8 Fit the crown around the head of a grown-up.
Now staple the crown shut. All done!
Your teacher is sure to be pleased.